Two Years and Two Months

poems by

Chris Reed

Finishing Line Press
Georgetown, Kentucky

Two Years and Two Months

With deepest thanks and with love
I dedicate this book to my mother
Frances Flowers
1921-2021

In June 2019, my mother, at ninety-eight years old, a widow and retired nurse, came up from North Carolina to live with me. During our two years and two months together, we experienced a time of healing memories and stories, the horrors and loneliness of the pandemic, and a world of ever stranger national politics.

During that time my mother had both a heart attack and a left frontal lobe event that messed with her memory. And during our time together, I started to write poetry.

As my mother lost the ability to read, I read aloud to her most afternoons. Among several classics her favorites were *Paradise Lost, Robinson Crusoe, Jane Eyre* and *Circe.*

Her last two months were in a nearby nursing facility where she died at the age of 100, in September 2021.

ACKNOWLEDGMENTS

I thank *New Verse News* for publishing "This Is Your Morning Briefing,"
and *U.S.1 Worksheets* for publishing "Gift."
In addition, thanks to *River Heron Review, New Verse News* and *Worksheets*
for the publication of several of my poems not included here.

Special thanks to two loving and encouraging mentors, Lois Harrod and Rice Lyons,
and to the "first reader" of most of these poems, Gabrielle Capoferri, for her greatly
valued feedback and encouragement.

Publisher: Leah Huete de Maines
Editor: Christen Kincaid
Cover Art: Joy Kreves
Author Photo: Chris Reed
Cover Design: Elizabeth Maines McCleavy

Order online: www.finishinglinepress.com
also available on amazon.com

Author inquiries and mail orders:
Finishing Line Press
PO Box 1626
Georgetown, Kentucky 40324
USA

Contents

Muse Mother in My Kitchen
June, 2019

Two rooms away, I try to write a poem.
My mother, in the kitchen, wrestles
a piece of toast out of the toaster,
that *just has never done this.*
She does it loudly, so I know
she's not disturbing my poem writing.

My mother, ninety-eight, still
a Catholic school girl, old age
bringing judgment, entitlement,
looking like wisdom to the untrained eye.
Her bent tenacity,
unguarded opinion-snatching,
her unsure smile channel
early Woody Allen.
She watches MSNBC most days,
latches onto an idea and runs with it.
I like that Bernie Sanders.
Is he married? Who is his wife?

My poem is warming.
I hear my mother at the kitchen table
scraping her toast, knife
dipping into the marmalade jar,
soft murmurs to her cat.
I look around for further inspiration,
see a book of Merwin poems—
visionary—saying all what is not,
for what actually is, cannot be spoken.

My mother calls out, *the coffee is not*
very hot this morning.
I imagine the tepid brown liquid,
knife-stirred, swirl in her cup.
I hear her frown to her cat knowingly.
My poem ponders coffee aroma,
toast crumbs on gnarled fingers,
cat's tongue caressing a pat of butter.
I stare at the Merwin book.

My mother—me.
What is, cannot be spoken.

Sky Prayer
July, 2019

look at that blue today
the wind and rain
have washed the sky clean
morning sunlight broadcasts
each detail of twig and leaf
every flutter of wing
lift of bill in song against
deep daylight blue
a black bird flies
smooth smudge
silken inkblot on the sky
my thanks to creation is this
that my mother and I sit here
eat breakfast
look out in awe
amen

My Mother's Feet

Your feet, bare, the story of your childhood
tosses you sprinting across the grass
after your shaggy black dog.
Gold morning sun, joy stretches your grin,
as you collapse on his soft neck.

An old photo illuminates adolescent feet
gripping mountain boulders,
a falls beside you, sparkles like youth.
With a shy smile, wide shorts, you lean,
balance on a precipice.

You tell me how you trampled in high boots,
portaging a canoe with your young husband,
through the grasses south of Selma.
You sidestep a diamondback, a quilter's cabin,
listen for the murmur of the Alabama in the mist.

I remember afternoons, your feet tapping,
knees crossed, you smoke at the kitchen table
with a backdoor neighbor.
Hospital shift over, kids, dinner waiting,
your laughter dances to a rhythm of discontent.

A grandmother, you move to a forgiving shore.
I visit and we walk mornings, heels, toes
sink into wet sand, footprints disappear
behind us. You focus on the water's edge,
sanderlings running before us.

Today your feet, red, swollen,
hard for you to reach, fit no shoes,
rest in plush pink socks on a worn recliner.
In stripes of late orange sun they unevenly
tap out dreams, wanderings they'll never tell.

Alice Journeys

I remind my mother of a beach in Georgia,
we were there when I was five,
the wet clay soil had pockets
that opened up and swallowed you.
My father struggled to save me,
my sister, my mother and himself.
He was afraid. I clawed
at the red slick and screamed.

I knew I was disappearing in that clay,
feeling hole into hole
open beneath me.
I didn't know what dying was,
my dog hadn't died yet.
Jesus, saints, and my grandfather
all died before I was born.

When my mother tries to remember
that beach, she sinks like Alice,
lands in her own childhood,
sliding down a slanted basement door
in the back of her house on Wood Road.
She picks splinters of green paint
from her fingers and clothes,

tells me her father would open that door,
cover the hole with quilts and leaves
at night, to catch thieves
who fell into the basement
trying to steal his bootleg liquor.
She laughs, they were always neighbors.
Above the hole I see her smile
against the windowpane.

Bumble

"...and the texture of life changes."
Elizabeth Kolbert, The Sixth Extinction

Fall goldenrod rides the field,
looks for bees in a late day sun
enlarged from western fires.
A honeybee mistakes my yellow
shirt swirling open.
Aging oaks drop indifferent leaves
orange, red, and brown,
now curling on my kitchen floor.

Remember the steamboat
at the end of Steamboat Road?
my mother asks. *I met a girl there*
who didn't have any shoes.
We were afraid of polio then,
and the concord grapes in the back
were covered with bees.

Afghan

remembering the afghan my mother crocheted after my father's death in 2009

From scraps of yarn my mother knits an afghan.
Her arthritic fingers work the remnants at dusk,
pale blue, pink, purple strands appear like bruises,
then a wash of gold, bandage against the blue.

Her arthritic fingers work the remnants. At dusk
my brother plays guitar, soft like my father's voice,
the sunset bandages the sky against a loss of blue.
Will night mask memories of wounded spirit?

My brother plays Bach on guitar, *a sotto voce*,
his wine, the deep red of my father's violence,
as darkness swathes memories of rent spirit.
What colors are you using now, Mother,

wine red, like my father's violence and pain?
Were these gnarled fingers meant to shield me?
What colors do you knit with now? My mother
ends a last strand, needles down, atonement.

Her gnarled fingers, meant to be my cover,
caress the blue, pink, purple strands, like bruises.
She hands me the afghan, needles down, atonement
in scraps of yarn. My mother knits an afghan.

Womansong: Cento
February 2020

I remember small things, flowers,
the bay coming in,
the lovers in an Irish story never had good fortune.
Why am I staring now,
hidden in dark folds of earth,
flowering shapes of fungus I could not know?
Look at the night sky,
the stars in a frozen arc overhead,
you'd swear that they were beds of irises.
Remember how they taught you once to pray?

I fell through a hole in the sky,
Humpty-Dumpty legs and arms.
The moon has nothing to be sad about,
her light is everywhere, remembering,
beautiful and faithful and ancient,
she lifts her brush once, like a thrown thing,
red edge of the moon,
or the fire of making new.

* Names of poems and poets in "Womansong" are found in the Notes
   on page 33

Milton in the Pandemic
April 2020

I read Milton aloud to my mother.
Angels and hosts of pagan gods
join history's winner, Jahweh.
Paradise Lost is not my choice
in this miasma of fear and oppression.
But my class was up to Satan rising
when the world constricted
and we now attend lectures on laptops.

A magnolia outside my window,
blue hepatica in the woods,
the lost archangel plots against
creation. His pain is that he
is removed from the source of love.
I wave to my granddaughter who
comes to run her dog. My mother
watches a news conference,
responds with tin sarcasm,
Yeah, I bet he does.

We turn back to Milton, but I can tell
my mother thinks it's blasphemous
to give Satan feelings, because she asks
Did anyone buy that book?
Meanwhile foxes cross the yard,
nuthatches visit the feeder, wildlife
expands with ease into eerie
vacated space, as Satan extols
God's creation, of which he is part.

I take a zoom yoga class, play cards
with my mother who always wins.
Milton moves on to Adam and Eve
who wrestle with the ivy growth,
while Satan finds his way over Chaos,
sneaks into the garden as a roaming mist.
The air is wet and my daughter and I
stay ten feet apart while we walk.

Eve falls for the same argument as Satan;
better to be independent and knowing,
than subservient and loved.
In zoom boxes we wonder
who made these mutually exclusive.
Swallows and bluebirds fight
over houses. Bluebirds are first but
swallows, better on the wing, win.

Adam and Eve renew their love, walk
in dust, knowing it as their final rest.
On a far cliff they look to a new world.
As I close the book, my mother,
perplexed by Milton, concedes,
I guess Satan wasn't really evil,
just too proud to say he was hurt.
My sister calls, she made a raspberry pie.

My Brother's Weekly Call
September 2020

Water retention.
My mother rests her legs on three pillows,
she names after Chekhov's title sisters,
Olga, Masha, and Irina.
Olga, sturdy and flat, just so,
Masha, next, gets folded in half,
slippery Irina wobbles on top.
Today, Sunday, she sits
with her legs on this V-shaped altar,
atop her home hospital bed,
to receive her son's weekly call.
Phone in hand, she sets her pained smile.

Hello, I'm still here, she offers
as prelude to her rhythmic summaries,
her *all in alls*, like Hail Mary's strung together.
All in all, we go nowhere now, with this virus.
All in all, I get up and use my walker some.
All in all, the world has changed,
and I don't understand it.
I can't read anymore or crochet.
I sometimes forget who you are.
All in all, I like the new square cookies
with my tea, and these socks
are nice and big,
and the birds, Jim,
the birds are at the feeder.

This Is Your Weekend Briefing
Sunday, November 15, 2020

My mother napped yesterday,
while I finished *Swann's Way*.
Her water retention is down,
and we hear that someone
is unlocking the secrets of aging.
There are no words for the U.S.
reaching eleven million cases
of coronavirus this morning,
although the eucharistic minister
wore a mask when she delivered
my mother's host earlier.

The bird feeders were filled today
and promptly visited by a finch
and a red-bellied woodpecker.
Currently we are recording
the Giants-Eagles game, in which
Daniel Jones and the Giants are
getting downfield, as constriction
threatens a transfer of power,
school reopenings and life itself.
I search for an artificial wreath.

We have some breaking news—
a stag is walking past the window,
and we are making the call
that he is at least four years old.
My mother sees him and reaches
for the word that means him,
although we still have no word
on reality out of the White House.
The Giants won this one. Enjoy
what remains of your weekend.

Christmas Count 2020

This Christmas we are just two,
myself and my 99-year old mother.
Eating almond strudel,
we miss an online church service,
ask Alexa to play *Adeste Fideles*.
We sing along, staying with verse one
drowning Pavarotti who knows all three.
I kick aside four riddle books,
finding a perfect riddle
for my five-year old grandson's text.
I considered the six-ton gorilla walking into
a movie theater, but developed
a visceral reaction to bullies this year.
My mother looks at channel seven,
for weather, wants to know
why it's raining on Christmas.
My brain is numb with daily numbers
of new infections and deaths.
I have eight texts: holiday greetings,
a photo, a late shipment notice,
and an ad for a concealed gun certificate.
I scroll over nine op-eds mostly on
the virus, one on the stress hormone
related to social isolation,
ignore the year-end attempts at humor,
study the ten best cookie recipes.
My mother says it's eleven, time for lunch,
I think there must be something,
a dozen of which could portend
a good new year.

Phantom
January 2021

You had a stroke, mom,
you're in the hospital,
but only for a few days.
Curled on your side
in a room that is both sunlit
and cold, you don't look up
at this stranger in a mask
allowed to visit for an hour.

Are you cold, Mom?
Your *no* encourages me,
as you tug at the bedspread,
short gentle movements,
holding it between your knuckles,
rhythmically smoothing it
with the side of your hand
after each tug.

At first I wonder if
you do this one-handed
because the hospital IV
goes into your other arm.
But there is something familiar
in this one-armed dance
of tug and smooth.

Then I hear your soft *come on,*
come on at each gentle tug,
and realize you speak to
your cat, making a place for her
on your lap, as you do
with her soft blanket,
in your chair at home.

I see how your face smooths
like the spread, how you
smile as you fold your arm
around her, your nose bending
down into her phantom fur,
both of you curling into
each other in the sun.

I Try to Write a Sonnet
January 2021

To start with, and I am not too upstream,
actually down in the fish splashing eddies,
my muse with pole is rebellious if anything.
She's knocking these prompts away with both
elbows, listening to voices downstairs.
I try for a pastorale while my mother
who had a stroke last week says "okay"
to the home health aide. Nails the consonant.
Crisp. But, still working on "yes" and "no."
My daughter swings in the kitchen door,
picking up laundry because her washer broke.
"Hi grandma." "Okay." It works.

I wade in, put my head back, fish nibble my toes.
The sky is high and I'm so downstream.

Spinach Pie

She gave me two of the peanut butter,
not the peanut butter,
fish.
No, the thing.
She gave me two of them
and I sent one back.
That was the feta spinach pie, Mom.
Who made that? Did you?
No. Trader Joes, but I put it in the oven.
I like fish.
It was spinach.
That's what I said, spinach.
Why do they keep talking?
Why don't they just go and vote?
Those are commentators talking about the vote.
It's a big deal. It's a run-off for the senate race
in Georgia.
Did she eat that other piece?
I don't know why they have all
these police and guards.
This is another story.
It's about a town in Wisconsin
where the police shot a man, Jacob Blake
in the back seven times.
They just announced
they're not going to charge the police
with a crime.
So people are angry.
Terrible … they should just vote.
Will you ask her about that other piece?

Gift

I watch my mother's ancient cat
with an existential question.
Yesterday she had a stroke,
sympathetic, to match my mother's,
and now refuses food and water.
Her right front leg and back left,
splay out as she tries to walk,
yet slowly she manages,
hugging the wall as she
makes her way around the house,
stopping at corners and baskets
for resting or hiding or leaving.
She lets us hold her, pet her,
though she can't jump up or down,
and has stopped mewing,
her purrs now too thin to feel.

My question is does a cat know?
Does she know about endings,
the finality of never hearing
someone's laughter again,
never seeing a story and feelings
told through the eyes, unique, gone?
Does she know about the flesh,
a dissolution that can't be
imagined, is mythically resisted.
Does she know this huge tragedy
that is the gift of life?
The leaving that starts on the day
we're born. To what end?
My mother holds her, hums
into the void. It's what we have.

Rhetorical Flourishes of a Left Frontal Lobe Event

1.
I learn the fine points of debate
from my post-stroke mother.

She asks Where were you?
Mom, I told you, I'd be upstairs
        for five minutes.
That's what I say, you were upstairs
        for five minutes.

2.
Learning rhetorical ambiguity.

She asks Did you feed the cat?
Yes. I always feed the cat.
Where's my good girl?

3.
Using repetition,
my mother surely not thinking of
"to die, to sleep,
to sleep, perchance to dream"

I'm ninety-nine years old.
        At ninety-nine years old,
        it's an outrage that I
        can't have bacon for breakfast.

4.
The above use of "outrage,"
a bonus lesson in hyperbole.

5.
As my mother turns 100,
she teaches slant, or a deeper truth.

Mom, here's your first happy 100th
        birthday card, *happy 100 years*
        young. It's from Anita,
        she's almost 98.

Isn't that amazing,
    that it got through,
    with all that mail,
    after all these years.

Coffee's Cold

As my daughter, an aide and I
share round-the-clock shifts,
this one tells me we don't need
the quilted bed pad, paper's enough.
That one says the urinary pad
doesn't need changing yet, it's dry.

Between this one and that one
the whole damn bed is wet
and I've been doing laundries
and Lysoling for three hours.
I'm working on a back spasm here
and you're telling me what?

Poetry for Breakfast

1. Expecting Something Reading Kay Ryan

Still on my first
cup of coffee,
I read *malice*
for *miracle*, look up
from the poem,
across the table,
and consider something
sinister behind
the frown
on your face
as you scrape
the jam jar
for its miracle
of one more knife
full of strawberries.

2. One Minute Please, I Just Want to Write

Lucille Clifton
wrote poems
as long as
her children's naps.
What kind of poems
can I write
between
your two cups
of coffee?

3. My Mother Discusses Kay Ryan

I watch as you
ignore my question
about the parable,
don't even hear it,
like grandma
conveniently
speaking only Polish.
You peer at the almost
empty jam jar,

intent on scraping
its last strawberry.

My question was
biblical, I thought
your cup of tea.
Your face, your hand
on the butter knife,
show no sign
of remembering
what the loaves
and fishes were.

But when I say *miracle*,
your shoulders ease
and you nod
in recognition.
Then, I realize,
as you add *please*,
you mean
another jar of jam.

Crumbs

Sitting in her wheelchair on the deck
this mild May morning
my mother has a new voice,
gravel-scratched and strong.
Eating her last Ritz cracker,
crumbs fall from her gnarled fingers
onto a clutched paper plate.
She regards my visiting brother,
my sister and myself with a gaze
that is confident and real.

Decades ago her voice was strong
in a different way, shrill, fear-driven,
needing to control children, husband,
needing to pretend that this
was what she wanted.
After her stroke, pieces of her past
collapsed against each other,
creating a new identity,
the person she wanted to be.
Now, no longer needing to pretend,
her voice is strong with genuine emotion.

She tells us she was seven or eight,
playing with children next door,
when the agent came to search for liquor.
He called to her and asked
if her father kept or sold any alcohol.
Her voice trembles with the fear
the child felt as she said no.
The agent asked what was in the shed
next to the garage. She said wood
and went to look.

And there he was, my father,
spread out, drunk. I closed the door
and was so afraid. I said no, just wood.
When he left I told my mother.
But my father, she says in a child's voice
mixing fear and anger,
he was an alcoholic, drinking

all the time, having debts,
buying illegal alcohol they tested
in the basement and sold to others.
You know, everyone respected him,
he was like a Polish godfather.
She shakes her head and says with
gravelly conviction, *but we knew,*
we knew he was sick,
we knew he was a drunk.

Her story unsettles us.
Before her stroke,
her father had been all good,
all providing, taking her to the farm
and gardens on the big estates.
letting her ride tractors and horses.
Several years ago, when we unearthed
his death certificate, stating
he suffered DTs in the hospital,
she said he'd had a drink that day.
We said you don't get DT's from a drink,
she pivoted to the clams he ate.

Is she now facing a truth of her past,
voicing an anger felt but unspoken,
as a child?
Or is she giving that little girl feelings
and knowledge that she never had?
We listen to her stories now,
as to a stranger, as she rewrites her self.
With no more fear or pretending,
she licks her finger
to pick up the last crumb.

Terrain

Using a walker my mother inches
to her recliner. Worn comfort launches
her back decades to a cityscape.
A wartime nurse, she crosses starlit
Central Park at night, coming home
from a shift at Flower Fifth.
Her breath slows as her bare feet
feel the cool pebbled beach where
before the war, she watched the spray
of girls water skiing, where
her father died from eating raw clams.

In her journey I am cast as her daughter,
her mother, a sister who wouldn't play,
the girl next door cleaning windows
until the dog bit her and the doctor came.
Her mind shifts over wide landscapes,
crashing continents into each other
to make new mountain ranges,
pulling them apart too quickly,
before oceans and shores can catch up.

Looking around for other terrain,
in slippered feet at the kitchen table
she asks *where am I?* I tell her the deer
are here eating the hydrangeas again.
She likes to watch them step through
the wild roses, comments on one
with a broken antler that comes alone.
Her tea beside her, she marks his slow time.
She is getting ready for her own
solo journey, I see her brace against
the scratch of the brambles.
She knows where she is.

Prospero

July 2021

To hear her tell it,
and you'd have to get up at 2:30
in the morning to do so,
you'd think dementia related to demons,
not etymologically,
but epistemologically.

Only when her mind lets the mirrors
slip a bit,
show what can't be seen head on,
after a wet bed accident,
being helped into dry clothes, sheets,
does she tell you there's a photographer
in the laundry room
taking pictures of this mess.

You glimpse her demons,
a flash of lizard tongue,
hear them creak out a word or two,
but they skitter and slither right back
to their spiny island nests
in her childhood.

In the morning with coffee,
mirrors back in place,
she asks is the marmalade new
and how did the green sheets
get on her bed.

Home

Stonebridge Nursing Facility, August 2021

In the end we all make a journey home,
alone, fitting into that space
that only we fit into.

My father, frail, even with a walker,
made it back to Selma, three days in my Honda.
He wanted to go home,
show me Ella White where he was born.
His sister said there's nothing there now,
only a crossroads.
In the end, smiling in a frown,
he was too weak to go that last bit.

My husband, after cancer, drove north to Canada,
to towns he'd visited summers,
his mother buying English china, Odawa baskets.
At Sault Ste. Marie, he dropped down
into Michigan through forests he'd known as a child,
past the dairy farm in Albion
where he played in the high loft.
Further west, he snuck up on Missoula,
and his wispy booze-laced poetry days.

I visit my mother now in this room,
not quite motel or hospital room or dorm.
One Zen moment to another.
We tell her she lives here now,
but this assurance for ourselves
doesn't go past the glasses she still wears.
On a journey of solitude,
she tries out the thinner air,
the empty spaces,
looks for the crossroads.

Passenger
Stonebridge, September 1, 2021

In the hills, my mother sits in a circle
with other grey-haired residents,
not understanding trivia questions
asked by a smiling aide.
I learn that today in 1914
the last passenger pigeon died
in a Cincinnati zoo.

The sun is strong this morning,
after tornadoes, flash floods,
torrents that have become expected,
a sun, strong, but no longer trustworthy,
ready to wrap itself
in some grey cape
of post-apocalyptic dust.

September first, a date learned
in school, not for the pigeon,
but Germany's invasion of Danzig,
the start of WWII.
These circled grey heads turning now
towards the barley soup, hoard
the last live memories of that war.

In the asphalt parking lot,
yesterday's heavy rain
still in sun-warmed puddles,
ignores how life retreats too quickly,
like the ocean between our toes,
trying to disappear smoothly,
unnoticed muted trickle

Ars Poetica

I look outside with finical hope,
but it's too hot for the sun to actually shine
in this heat wave. A soft jazz piano
rides the hum of the window air conditioner
as a resident in her wheelchair rolls past
the doorway in one direction,
while a mop makes tight circles
going the other way.
My mother sleeps with eyes that flutter,
her head tilted on the pillow,
ready to sit upright
at the first sound of a tuna sandwich
and sliced peaches listing down the hall.
Our own Faustian bargain,
poets and muses don't need the profound,
just hums and tilts.

Timbre

Your syllables flutter like feathers,
the thought that sends them aloft
bends your neck toward me, just a bit.
I pluck some from the air
try to recognize a pattern
see your meaning.
Your eyes work to focus,
look for a cadence to ride.
I say *it's okay*, my hand rests
on the cool flesh of skeletal fingers,
your knuckles.
We communicate through the bone.

Untitled

September 20, 2021

the road to those last minutes is narrow
tree-lined
I tell the trees they will never be the same
when I drive home
the loss of you will surely leave space
the air press differently on my skin
light be more porous
not hold together

your heart still beats
but your breath erratic
considering
your jaw slack mouth open
its dark circle framed by blackened lips
hands purple already cold
I place a drop of water on your lip
you don't swallow
your fingers wrap around three of mine
as a baby does

no holy water no pope blessed rosary
mother of pearl crucifix from Jerusalem
in the end a simple incantation
a thank you a kiss goodbye
truth flowing through the skin
of our joined hands
that this journey is a return
a going home
that your love in its myriad forms endures

you stay with me don't leave
on my way home I stop at the market
for paper towels
when they call me back
to say you've gone I clutch
our mother daughter love
complicated many stranded
a cool finger wrap
the coming sunset already so orange
I forget to notice the trees

September Morning

Coarse drapes slide open,
soft mist covers the morning,
palls the early sun.

A pale green maple leaf
spirals to the cedar deck,
defiant yellow streaks.

Thank you for the scones.
A ghost moves in the kitchen,
crumbs on my fingers.

Cream clots slowly swirl
on the surface of my tea,
morning clouds disappear.

Milkweed pods crack open,
bundles of white flossy seeds
look toward a fall breeze.

Warm air lifts the scent
of woody rosemary stalks,
untended garden.

Soft flutter of wings,
an olive warbler vanishes
into orange weeds.

Seasons balance on a fulcrum.
I reach for your curled form,
on high, a soaring crane.

Still Life
Fall 2021

A plastic bag of mom's old pills,
a four pack of toilet paper beside
the box of dad's ashes
with his photo on top, the one
of him in a wheelchair smiling,
and mom's small statue of Mary
holding down a wrinkled shopping list
that ends in celery, cereal, grapes,
sit in the thin dust that's visible
only in the morning sun,
atop the old dresser that's missing
two drawer pulls, the dresser
we thought was an antique.

Two circle drums whose deep rhythms
lifted me to dance on shadows,
hang on the wall behind the dresser,
peer out at me,
as the sun leaves
and the dust disappears.

Notes

The lines in "Womansong: Cento" are from the following poets and poems:

Louise Glück : Vespers
Elizabeth Bishop : The Moose
Eavan Boland : Once
Wislava Szymborska: Astonishment
Susan Ludvigson : Trinity
Keetje Kuipers : River Sonnet
Glück : Spring Snow
Boland : Lines for a 30 wedding anniversary
Bishop : Crusoe in England
Tracy Smith : Solstice

Joy Harjo : 4 Songs
Kay Ryan : Simply by Growing Larger
Sylvia Plath : Edge
Sappho #43
Lucille Clifton : In Praise of Menstruation
Adrienne Rich : She
Clifton : In Praise of Menstruation
Ruth Padel: To the Distant Beloved

As a minister with a focus on social justice issues, **Chris Reed** worked with the poetry and music of worship, ceremony, prayers, sermons, eulogies and spiritual writings, including developing and writing a guide for interfaith visits, Neighboring Faiths, Skinner House. She served the Unitarian Universalist Congregation of Princeton for 22 years and as UU Chaplain at Princeton University for ten years.

Given retirement, her aging mother, the covid pandemic and a life-long love of literature, she turned to reading and writing poetry to find meaning amid loss and confusion, and to celebrate our moments and actions that are life-affirming.

www.ingramcontent.com/pod-product-compliance
Lightning Source LLC
Chambersburg PA
CBHW020222090426
42734CB00008B/1181